Fannie Mae's and Freddie Mac's Financial Problems

N. Eric Weiss
Specialist in Financial Economics

August 10, 2012

Congressional Research Service
7-5700
www.crs.gov
RL34661

CRS Report for Congress
Prepared for Members and Committees of Congress

Summary

The continuing conservatorship of Fannie Mae and Freddie Mac at a time of uncertainty in the housing, mortgage, and financial markets has raised doubts about the future of these enterprises, which are chartered by Congress as government-sponsored enterprises (GSEs) and whose debts are widely believed to be implicitly guaranteed by the federal government.

In the second quarter of 2012, both Fannie Mae and Freddie Mac reported profits for the first time since the fourth quarter of 2006. Also, the second quarter of 2012 was first time that neither GSE had to request financial support from the Treasury.

The Treasury has agreed to buy mortgage-backed securities (MBSs) from the GSEs and to raise funds for them. Initially, each GSE gave Treasury $1 billion in senior preferred stock and warrants to acquire, at nominal cost, 80% of each GSE. Treasury holds more than $187 billion of preferred stock in the two GSEs. Treasury has agreed to invest whatever is required to maintain GSE solvency through calendar year 2012. Now the formerly implicit guarantee is nearly explicit. In addition to Treasury's purchases of senior preferred stock, the Federal Reserve (Fed) has purchased GSE bonds and MBSs.

Under terms of the federal government's purchase of their preferred stock, the enterprises are required to pay the government dividends of nearly $20 billion annually (10% of the support). Housing, mortgage, and even general financial markets remain in an unprecedented situation.

Estimates of the total cost to the federal government use different baselines and vary widely. The FHFA estimates that Treasury is likely to purchase $220 billion-$311 billion of senior preferred stock by the end of 2014. The Congressional Budget Office estimates the budget cost to be more than $300 billion. Standard & Poor's has estimated the cost at $280 billion plus $405 billion to create a replacement system.

Once Treasury's support for Fannie Mae and Freddie Mac ends, sometime after 2012, the GSEs will be challenged to pay the 10% annual cash dividend contained in their contracts. The enterprises could instead pay a 12% annual senior preferred stock dividend indefinitely.

In August 2011, Standard & Poor's downgraded the debt of the federal government, Fannie Mae, and Freddie Mac. To date, there is no evidence that this has increased mortgage interest rates, but the impact may take longer to occur or to be detected.

Legislation introduced in the 112th Congress, the future of the GSEs, and ways to reduce the cost to the federal government are analyzed in CRS Report R41822, *Proposals to Reform Fannie Mae and Freddie Mac in the 112th Congress*, by N. Eric Weiss.

Contents

Introduction 1
Fannie Mae's and Freddie Mac's Current Status 1
    What Is the Current Financial Condition of Fannie Mae and Freddie Mac? 1
    What is the Likely Impact of Standard & Poor's Downgrade of the Federal
        Government, Fannie Mae, and Freddie Mac? 5
    Can the GSEs Continue to Pay Dividends to Treasury? 5
    Is the Government Investigating Fannie Mae and Freddie Mac? 6
    Why Did Fannie Mae Attempt to Sell Low-Income Housing Tax Credits? 6
    What Is Happening to Fannie Mae's and Freddie Mac's Affordable Housing
        Initiatives? 7
    Do Fannie Mae and Freddie Mac Have Any Programs to Help Mortgage Borrowers? 7
    Who Manages the GSEs? 8
    What Is Happening to Executive Compensation? 8
    What Risks Do Fannie Mae's and Freddie Mac's Financial Problems Create for
        Homeowners and Those Planning to Become Homeowners? 9
    What Risks Do Fannie Mae and Freddie Mac Face in Today's Economic
        Environment? 9
    What Is the Federal Government's Potential Contribution? 10
    What Risks Do Fannie Mae and Freddie Mac Create for the U.S. Government? 12
    What is the Difference Between the Housing and Economic Recovery Act of 2008
        and the Federal Housing Finance Regulatory Reform Act of 2008? 12
Future 13
    Could the GSEs Continue as Before? 13
    What Are Some of Congress's Options for Restructuring the GSEs? 13
    What Has Conservatorship Done to Stockholders and Other Stakeholders? 14
    How Can Fannie Mae and Freddie Mac Leave Conservatorship? 15
Context 15
    What Is Conservatorship? 15
    Why Did the FHFA Place Fannie Mae and Freddie Mac Under Conservatorship? 16
    What Was Fannie Mae's and Freddie Mac's Financial Position? 16
    Why Did Fannie Mae's and Freddie Mac's Stock Prices Decline in 2008? 17
    Why Did FHFA Act on September 7, 2008, Instead of Earlier or Later? 17
    Are There Precedents for Placing Fannie Mae and Freddie Mac Under
        Conservatorship? 18
    Who Heads FHFA? 18
    What Has Congress Done Previously to Improve the Financial Condition of the
        GSEs? 18
    What Other Actions Has the Federal Government Taken to Address the Financial
        Condition of the GSEs? 19
    Who Has Invested in the GSEs? 20
    What Recent Legislation Has Affected the GSEs? 20
Glossary 22

Tables

Table 1. GSE Profitability Since 2006 2
Table 2. Treasury Holdings of GSE Senior Preferred Stock 4
Table 3. GSE 2010-2014 Housing Goals and Subgoals 7
Table 4. Public Laws Specifically Affecting GSEs 21

Contacts

Author Contact Information 22

Introduction

This report presents, in analytical question and answer form, the issues surrounding the financial conditions of Fannie Mae and Freddie Mac, which are stockholder-owned government-sponsored enterprises (GSEs). Their federal charters give the GSEs special public policy goals aimed at providing liquidity in the mortgage market and to provide access to homeownership for underserved groups and locations. In return, their charters give the GSEs a special relationship with the government.

On September 7, 2008, the federal government took control of the GSEs from their stockholders and management in a process known as conservatorship. The goal of conservatorship is to restore the GSEs' financial strength and to return control to their stockholders and management. Conservatorship is discussed in more detail later in this report.

A glossary of terms is included at the end of this report.

Fannie Mae's and Freddie Mac's Current Status

What Is the Current Financial Condition of Fannie Mae and Freddie Mac?

The second quarter of 2012 was the first time that Fannie Mae and Freddie Mac reported profits since the end of 2006. **Table 1** summarizes the losses and profits of Fannie Mae and Freddie Mac since 2006. Since 2007, neither GSE has reported a profitable year.

The second quarter of 2012 was also the first time that neither GSE had to request financial support from the Treasury (see **Table 2**).

The GSEs' losses that started in late 2006 are notable because previously the GSEs had been consistently profitable. Fannie Mae had not reported a full-year loss since 1985, and Freddie Mac had never reported a full-year loss since it became stockholder owned.[1]

---

[1] Federal Housing Finance Agency, *Report to Congress: 2011*, pp. 72 and 89, available at http://www.fhfa.gov/webfiles/24009/FHFA_RepToCongr11_6_14.pdf, hereafter referred to as FHFA.

Table 1. GSE Profitability Since 2006

($ in millions)

Quarter	Fannie Mae	Freddie Mac
1st Quarter 2006	$2,026	$1,942
2nd Quarter 2006	2,058	1,336
3rd Quarter 2006	-629	-550
4th Quarter 2006	604	401
Full Year 2006	**4,059**	**2,327**
1st Quarter 2007	961	-133
2nd Quarter 2007	1,947	729
3rd Quarter 2007	-1,399	-1,238
4th Quarter 2007	-3,559	-2,452
Full Year 2007	**-2,050**	**-3,094**
1st Quarter 2008	-2,186	-151
2nd Quarter 2008	-2,300	-821
3rd Quarter 2008	-28,994	-25,295
4th Quarter 2008	-25,227	-23,852
Full Year 2008	**-58,707**	**-50,119**
1st Quarter 2009	-23,168	-9,975
2nd Quarter 2009	-14,754	302
3rd Quarter 2009	-18,872	-5,408
4th Quarter 2009	-15,175	-6,472
Full Year 2009	**-71,969**	**-21,553**
1st Quarter 2010	-11,530	-6,688
2nd Quarter 2010	-1,218	-4,713
3rd Quarter 2010	-1,339	-2,511
4th Quarter 2010	73	-113
Full Year 2010	**-14,014**	**-14,025**
1st Quarter 2011	-6,471	676
2nd Quarter 2011	-2,893	-2,139
3rd Quarter 2011	-5,085	-4,422
4th Quarter 2011	-2,406	619
Full Year 2011	**-16,855**	**-5,266**
1st Quarter 2012	2,719	577
2nd Quarter 2012	4,114	3,020

Source: Fannie Mae (http://www.fanniemae.com/ir/) and Freddie Mac (http://www.freddiemac.com/investors/er).

Note: Freddie Mac's 2009 annual report revised previously released 2009 quarterly net income. This table reflects the revisions. Amounts shown are "net loss attributable to Fannie Mae," and "net loss attributable to

Freddie Mac," which exclude dividends paid to Treasury on the senior preferred stock. All other dividends have been suspended.

Two major sources of losses for mortgage lenders, including the GSEs, have been loans to borrowers with less than prime credit (subprime) and certain types of mortgages to borrowers with credit between prime and subprime (Alt-A). At the end of 2011, Fannie Mae held $16.6 billion in private-label mortgage-backed securities (MBSs) backed by subprime mortgages; it held $19.7 billion in private-label MBSs backed by Alt-A mortgages.[2] Freddie Mac held $49.0 billion in private-label MBSs backed by subprime mortgages and $16.8 billion in private-label MBSs backed by Alt-A mortgages.[3] The GSEs have, in addition, increased loan loss reserves in anticipation of continuing losses. If losses on foreclosed mortgages are less than predicted, the reserves could be reduced, which would improve the GSEs' financial condition.

To make certain that the GSEs have adequate funds to cover potential losses, the Federal Housing Finance Agency (FHFA), like all financial safety and soundness regulators, imposes capital requirements. At the end of 2007, the two GSEs had a surplus of $24.8 billion more than the regulatory capital requirement of $58.4 billion; they had a surplus of $50.8 billion more than the risk-based capital requirement of $38.8 billion.[4] At the end of 2011, Fannie Mae had a minimum capital requirement deficit of $148.4 billion and Freddie Mac had minimum capital requirement deficit of $88.7 billion.[5] FHFA has said that it will not calculate risk based capital requirements while the GSEs are in conservatorship.

To meet their capital requirements, the GSEs could either reduce their needed capital by selling some mortgages and MBSs from their portfolios, or raise new capital from investors. They have been unable or unwilling to take either alternative. Instead, they have sold additional preferred stock to the Treasury.

Since the third quarter of 2008, FHFA, as conservator of the GSEs, has asked Treasury for a total of $116.1 billion to increase Fannie Mae's assets to offset its liabilities and a total of $71.3 billion for Freddie Mac.[6] Technically, Treasury support for the GSEs comes through purchases of GSE senior preferred stock. **Table 2** reports the amounts, including the $1 billion of senior preferred stock that each GSE gave Treasury when they were taken into conservatorship. This stock is senior to (has priority over) all other common and preferred stock; it is the only stock currently receiving dividends.

---

[2] FHFA, p. 78.

[3] FHFA, p. 95.

[4] FHFA, p. 83 and 100. Regulatory capital is based on the amount of mortgages that a GSE has purchased. Risk-based capital is based on the riskiness of the mortgages a GSE has purchased. A GSE must have enough capital to meet the greater of these two amounts.

[5] FHFA, pp. 121 and 138.

[6] FHFA, "Data as of June 20, 2012 on Treasury and Federal Reserve Purchase Programs for GSE and Mortgage-Related Securities," http://www.fhfa.gov/webfiles/24022/TSYSupport%202012-06-20.pdf.

Table 2. Treasury Holdings of GSE Senior Preferred Stock

($ in millions)

	Fannie Mae	Freddie Mac
Initial Agreement (No explicit cost)	$1,000	$1,000
3rd Quarter 2008	0	13,800
4th Quarter 2008	15,200	30,800
Year 2008	**16,200**	**45,600**
1st Quarter 2009	19,000	6,100
2nd Quarter 2009	10,700	0
3rd Quarter 2009	15,000	0
4th Quarter 2009	15,300	0
Year 2009	**60,000**	**6,100**
1st Quarter 2010	8,400	10,600
2nd Quarter 2010	1,500	1,800
3rd Quarter 2010	2,500	100
4th Quarter 2010	2,600	500
Year 2010	**15,000**	**13,000**
1st Quarter 2011	8,500	0
2nd Quarter 2011	5,087	1,479
3rd Quarter 2011	7,791	5,992
4th Quarter 2011	4,571	146
Year 2011	**25,949**	**7,617**
1st Quarter 2012	0	19
2nd Quarter 2012	0	0
Total Holdings	**$117,149**	**$72,336**

Source: Fannie Mae (http://www.fanniemae.com/ir/), Freddie Mac (http://www.freddiemac.com/investors/er/), and FHFA (http://www.fhfa.gov/Default.aspx?Page=70).

Note: Each "total holdings" includes $1 billion in senior preferred stock that the GSEs gave Treasury at the time of their conservatorship agreements. Except for the first draw, Treasury has actually paid the GSEs on the last day of the next quarter: March 31, June 30, September 30, and December 31.

In addition to Treasury's purchases of senior preferred stock, the Federal Reserve (Fed) has purchased GSE bonds and MBSs. In programs that started in September 2008 and ended in March 2010, together the Fed and Treasury purchased $1,135.9 billion in MBSs.[7] On September 21, 2011, the Fed decided to begin reinvesting MBS principal repayments in other MBSs.[8] As of

---

[7] U.S. Federal Housing Finance Agency, "Data as of June 10, 2012, on Treasury and Federal Reserve Purchase Programs for GSE and Mortgage-Related Securities," http://www.fhfa.gov/webfiles/24022/TSYSupport%202012-06-20.pdf.

[8] Federal Reserve Bank of New York, "FAQs: Reinvestments of Principal Payments on Agency Securities into Agency MBS," September 26, 2011, http://www.newyorkfed.org/markets/ambs/ambs_faq.html.

the end of the second quarter of 2012, the Fed held $855.0 billion of Fannie Mae's and Freddie Mac's MBSs.[9]

What is the Likely Impact of Standard & Poor's Downgrade of the Federal Government, Fannie Mae, and Freddie Mac?

On August 5, 2011, Standard & Poor's (S&P), a nationally recognized statistical rating organization, downgraded its rating of the federal government's debt by one level from AAA to AA+.[10] On August 8, 2011, S&P cited Fannie Mae's and Freddie Mac's dependence on the federal government's support and downgraded them from AAA to AA+.[11] It is not clear what the impact of these downgrades will be on mortgage interest rates. The other two large ratings agencies, Moody's and Fitch, have reaffirmed their current AAA rating for the United States.

Normally, borrowers with lower credit ratings pay higher interest rates, but it is not clear if this will hold for the federal government and on mortgage interest rates. The downgrade reflects a change from an "extremely strong capacity to meet its financial commitments" to a "very strong" capacity. This rating change might be offset by other factors such as the huge size of the market for U.S. Treasuries, economic and financial problems within the Economic and Monetary Union in Europe and elsewhere, and general changes in the world's economies.

Freddie Mac conducts a weekly primary mortgage market survey® (PMMS®) that reported an initial drop in mortgage interest rates. The August 4, 2011, reported rate on a 30-year, fixed-rate mortgage was 4.39% and the reported rate a week later (August 11, 2011) was slightly lower at 4.32%.[12] The rate reported for July 12, 2012, was 3.56%.

Can the GSEs Continue to Pay Dividends to Treasury?

Under terms of the support contracts that the GSEs individually signed with Treasury, each is required to pay annually either 10% cash dividends or 12% stock dividends on the senior preferred stock issued to Treasury. As of the second quarter of 2012, this requires Fannie Mae to pay annually either $11.7 billion in cash or $14.1 billion in stock and Freddie Mac to pay either $7.2 billion in cash or $8.6 billion in stock. Fannie Mae has never earned enough in any single year to make such large dividend payments in cash; Freddie Mac earned enough only once—in 2002.[13] Consequently, once the GSEs no longer are receiving financial support from Treasury, the GSEs would have to be more profitable than they ever have been for them to make more than one year of cash dividend payments. This is made less likely by provisions in the contracts requiring the GSEs to reduce the size of their mortgage portfolios, which in recent years the GSEs increased to increase their profits.

---

[9] Federal Reserve Bank of New York, "System Open Market Account Holdings: Securities Holdings as of June 27, 2012," http://www.newyorkfed.org/markets/soma/sysopen_accholdings.html.

[10] See CRS Report R41955, *Standard & Poor's Downgrade of U.S. Government Long-Term Debt*, by Mark Jickling for more information about the downgrade.

[11] S&P also downgraded their rating of 10 of the 12 Federal Home Loan Banks to AA+. The other two Federal Home Loan Banks were already rated AA+.

[12] Freddie Mac, *Weekly Primary Mortgage Market Survey (PMMS)*, http://www.freddiemac.com/pmms/.

[13] U.S. Federal Housing Finance Agency, *Report to Congress: 2010*, pages 114 and 131, available at http://www.fhfa.gov/webfiles/21572/FHFA2010_RepToCongress6_13_11.pdf.

Without Treasury's support, a GSE lacking the funds to pay the cash dividend could pay the 12% dividend in additional senior preferred stock. It appears that this could continue indefinitely unless Congress were to pass legislation modifying the GSE's charter, Treasury were to take control of the GSE by exercising its warrants to purchase 79.9% of the GSE's common stock, or FHFA as conservator were to act.

Is the Government Investigating Fannie Mae and Freddie Mac?

Investigations are confidential, but there have been media reports that the Securities and Exchange Commission (SEC) is investigating several current or former GSE executives.[14] SEC is reported to have sent formal notice of its intent to recommend civil charges against former Fannie Mae chief executive officer (CEO) Daniel H. Mudd, former Freddie Mac CEO Richard F. Syron, former Freddie Mac chief financial officer Anthony S. Piszel, and Freddie Mac executive vice president Donald J. Bisenius. These notices (known as Wells notices) provide the opportunity to respond to the charges and to persuade the SEC not to proceed with the recommendation to the commission to file civil charges.

Why Did Fannie Mae Attempt to Sell Low-Income Housing Tax Credits?

Fannie Mae's quarterly report for the third quarter of 2009 reported that the company was seeking the government's permission to sell approximately $2.6 billion in Low-Income Housing Tax Credits (LIHTC). The credits had little or no value to Fannie Mae because the GSE is not likely to incur any tax liabilities in the foreseeable future. FHFA approved the sale as consistent with ongoing efforts to "conserve Enterprise assets and with the Enterprise's multifamily housing mission."[15] Under its senior preferred stock agreement, Fannie Mae was required to obtain Treasury's approval to dispose of these assets. Treasury denied the request as being too costly for taxpayers: Fannie Mae is very unlikely to earn enough income to pay taxes, making the tax credits useless to Fannie Mae and costless to Treasury.[16] Any company purchasing the credits would do so to reduce its taxes, reducing Treasury's tax revenues.

Freddie Mac has stated that in light of the Treasury decision about Fannie Mae, it will not request permission to sell its LIHTC.[17]

---

[14] Ben Protess and Azam Ahmed, "Ex-Chief of Freddie May Face Civil Action," *The New York Times*, March 16, 2011, p. B1.

[15] U.S. Federal Housing Finance Agency, "Statement of FHFA Acting Director Edward J. DeMarco Concerning the Possible Transfer of Fannie Mae Low-Income Housing Tax Credits to Investors," press release, November 5, 2009, http://www.fhfa.gov/webfiles/15169/LIHTC%20statement%2011%205%2009%20final.pdf.

[16] Federal National Mortgage Association, *Securities and Exchange Commission Form 8-K*, November 6, 2009, available at http://edgar.sec.gov/Archives/edgar/data/310522/000129993309004466/htm_35059.htm.

[17] Federal Home Loan Mortgage Corporation, *Securities and Exchange Commission Form 10-K,* February 11, 2010, available at http://www.freddiemac.com/investors/er/pdf/10k_022410.pdf.

What Is Happening to Fannie Mae's and Freddie Mac's Affordable Housing Initiatives?

The Housing and Economic Recovery Act of 2008 (HERA; P.L. 110-289) gives the FHFA authority to set housing goals for Fannie Mae and Freddie Mac. **Table 3** summarizes the 2010 to 2014 housing goals and subgoals. Fannie Mae and Freddie Mac can also meet a housing goal or subgoal by purchasing sufficient qualifying mortgages to mirror or exceed the market.

Table 3. GSE 2010-2014 Housing Goals and Subgoals

Category	2010-2011 Actual Goal	2012-1014 Proposed Goal
Low-Income Families Housing Goal (Fannie Mae, Freddie Mac)	27% purchase money	20% purchase money
Very Low-Income Families Housing Goal (Fannie Mae, Freddie Mac)	8% purchase money	7% purchase money
Low-Income Areas Housing Goal (Fannie Mae, Freddie Mac)	13% purchase money	11% purchase money
Refinancing Housing Goal (Fannie Mae, Freddie Mac)	21% refinance	21% refinance
Multifamily Low-Income Housing Goal (Fannie Mae)	177,750 dwelling units	2012: 251,000 dwelling units 2013: 245,000 dwelling units 2014: 223,000 dwelling units
Multifamily Low-Income Housing Goal (Freddie Mac)	161,250 dwelling units	2012: 191,000 dwelling units 2013: 203,000 dwelling units 2014: 181,000 dwelling units
Multifamily Very Low-Income Housing Subgoal (Fannie Mae)	42,750 dwelling units	2012: 60,000 dwelling units 2013: 59,000 dwelling units 2014: 53,000 dwelling units
Multifamily Very Low-Income Housing Subgoal (Freddie Mac)	21,000 dwelling units	2012: 32,000 dwelling units 2013: 31,000 dwelling units 2014: 27,000 dwelling units

Sources: U.S. Federal Housing Finance Agency, "2010–2011 Enterprise Housing Goals; Enterprise Book-entry Procedures," 75 *Federal Register* 55892-55939, September 14, 2010; U.S. Federal Housing Finance Agency, "2012-2014 Enterprise Housing Goals," 77 *Federal Register*, June 11, 2012, 34263-34281.

Notes: Alternatively, Fannie Mae and Freddie Mac can meet their housing goals by purchasing mortgages to equal or exceed the market percentage. "Purchase money" mortgages are mortgages used to purchase a house as opposed to refinance a house that is already owned.

Do Fannie Mae and Freddie Mac Have Any Programs to Help Mortgage Borrowers?

Fannie Mae[18] and Freddie Mac[19] each have special programs for mortgage borrowers, but only for borrowers whose loans each holds. These programs include allowing certain borrowers who

---

[18] Fannie Mae, "Avoiding Foreclosure," available at http://www.fanniemae.com/portal/helping-homeowners-communities/foreclosure-help.html.

[19] Freddie Mac, "Alternatives to Foreclosure," http://www.freddiemac.com/avoidforeclosure/alternatives_to_foreclosure.html.

owe more than their homes are currently worth to refinance their mortgages or enter into repayment plans, forbearance plans, mortgage modifications, and deed-for-lease[20] plans. There are also plans to avoid foreclosure through short sales and deeds-in-lieu of foreclosure.

Fannie Mae and Freddie Mac have programs to allow a homeowner facing foreclosure to surrender the deed in lieu of foreclosure and then to lease the home back. The Fannie Mae lease is for 12 months and can be renewed, whereas the Freddie Mac lease is month-to-month. Both programs charge a market rate for the lease.

The GSEs' refinance programs differ in terms of interest rates and fees.

The Home Affordable Loan Modification program is for borrowers who are delinquent on their mortgages. The Home Affordable Refinance is for borrowers who are current on their mortgages and want to refinance to a lower interest rate. Both programs have certain eligibility and qualification requirements. The programs are being administered by the borrower's current mortgage servicer.[21]

Who Manages the GSEs?

Fannie Mae and Freddie Mac have separate management teams headed by a chief executive officer and overseen by their conservator and regulator, the Federal Housing Finance Agency. Fannie Mae CEO Daniel H. Mudd and Freddie Mac CEO Richard F. Syron resigned when their companies were placed in conservatorship on September 7, 2008. FHFA appointed Herbert M. Allison, Jr. as Fannie Mae's CEO and David Moffett as Freddie Mac's CEO.

Effective March 13, 2009, Moffett resigned from Freddie Mac to return to the private sector. He has since returned as a consultant. On April 20, 2009, Allison resigned from Fannie Mae to accept the nomination to be Assistant Treasury Secretary for Financial Stability (who oversees Treasury's Troubled Asset Relief Program) and Counselor to the Secretary.

On May 10, 2012, Freddie Mac appointed Donald H. Layton as CEO effective May 21.[22] On June 5, 2012, Fannie Mae appointed Timothy J. Mayopoulos as CEO effective June 18.[23]

What Is Happening to Executive Compensation?

The Housing and Economic Recovery Act (HERA; P.L. 110-289) strengthened FHFA's regulation over executive compensation and so-called golden parachutes. The senior preferred stock agreement signed by each GSE with FHFA requires the GSEs to get approval for new

---

[20] In a deed-for-lease plan, the delinquent homeowner surrenders the deed to the lender and leases (rents) the home for an agreed upon time period.

[21] Information on these programs is available at http://www.makinghomeaffordable.gov/.

[22] Federal Home Loan Mortgage Corporation, "Form 8-K," May 10, 2012, available at http://www.sec.gov/Archives/edgar/data/1026214/000102621412000051/f71884e8vk.htm.

[23] Federal National Mortgage Association, "Form 8-K," June 5, 2012, available at http://www.sec.gov/Archives/edgar/data/310522/000129993312001410/htm_45294.htm.

compensation agreements with executives. The current CEOs each are receiving salaries of $600,000.[24]

What Risks Do Fannie Mae's and Freddie Mac's Financial Problems Create for Homeowners and Those Planning to Become Homeowners?

Fannie Mae's and Freddie Mac's financial problems create no risks for homeowners who want to stay in their homes and who do not want to refinance. Homeowners continue to pay their existing mortgages.

Treasury's actions of lending money to the GSEs and the Fed's purchases of the GSEs' MBSs appear to have helped to stabilize the secondary mortgage market and provided a continuing flow of funds to purchase new homes and to refinance existing mortgages. In 2007, the GSEs financed 91.3% of the conforming mortgage market, and their 2008 market share was 97.8%.[25] In 2009 and 2010, the share of the GSEs combined with Federal Housing Administration (FHA) has been over 90%.[26]

Under conservatorship, the GSEs have become active in loan modifications and refinancing existing mortgages that they own. They have become more cautious about the mortgages that they purchase, with stricter underwriting rules and higher fees. These actions are similar to other lenders' behavior in the recent recession and in previous economic slowdowns.

The Economic Stimulus Act of 2008 (ESA) raised the loan limit for FHA guaranteed loans in most high-cost areas of the nation to the same maximum that the GSEs are permitted to purchase.[27] As a result, FHA-guaranteed loans can, in theory, replace most conventional mortgages.

What Risks Do Fannie Mae and Freddie Mac Face in Today's Economic Environment?

In any economic environment, Fannie Mae and Freddie Mac face a variety of risks that many other companies face. The GSEs purchase home mortgages. They package most mortgages into MBSs, selling some and holding others in their investment portfolios. The GSEs finance their portfolios of long-term (typically 30-year) mortgages with short-term borrowing (typically three

---

[24] Federal National Mortgage Association, "Form 8-K," June 5, 2012, available at http://www.sec.gov/Archives/edgar/data/310522/000129993312001410/0001299933-12-001410.txt, and Federal Home Loan Mortgage Corporation, "Form 8-K," May 10, 2012, available at http://www.sec.gov/Archives/edgar/data/1026214/000102621412000051/f71884e8vk.htm.

[25] *The 2008 Mortgage Market Statistical Annual*, Volume II (Bethesda, MD: Inside Mortgage Finance Publications, 2008), pp. 3, 9 and *The 2009 Mortgage Market Statistical Annual*, Volume II (Bethesda, MD: Inside Mortgage Finance Publications, 2009), pp. 3, 9. A conforming mortgage is one that is under the conforming loan limit, which is as high as $729,750 in high-cost areas.

[26] U.S. Department of the Treasury and Department of Housing and Urban Development, "Reforming America's Housing Finance Market: A Report to Congress," February 2011, p. 12, available at http://www.treasury.gov/initiatives/Documents/Reforming%20America%27s%20Housing%20Finance%20Market.pdf.

[27] P.L. 110-185, 122 Stat. 613 et seq.

months to five years). This increases the GSEs' profits because short-term borrowing is usually less expensive than longer term loans. At the same time, this creates *interest rate risk*, which is the risk that if short-term interest rates increase, profitability can be reduced or can even turn to losses. For example, if interest rates were to increase to 6%, mortgages at 5% would not be profitable.[28] To try to reduce these risks, the GSEs use a variety of financial derivatives.[29]

The Federal Reserve has said that it will hold interest rates low through 2014 and that it would attempt to lower longer-term interest rates.[30] In the short run, this could aid the GSEs: they finance mortgages by borrowing for relatively short periods of time and will be able to borrow at lower interest rates. In the longer run when interest rates increase, the GSEs' profitability may be challenged as they refinance their short-term borrowing at rates that could be greater than what they receive on their mortgages.

In a worst-case scenario, the interest rate on short-term loans to the GSEs could increase enough to cause substantial losses and investors could stop entering into derivative contracts with the GSEs. This would leave the GSEs, who anticipated being able to roll over their short-term debt, unable to refinance.

The GSEs are also subject to *credit risk*. The GSEs guarantee timely payment of principal and interest of the mortgages in their MBSs. As mortgage foreclosure rates have climbed since 2006, and as home prices have fallen, the value of the mortgages and MBSs that the two firms hold in their portfolio has also fallen. Uncertainty about the duration and severity of the housing slump means that markets cannot now gauge the riskiness of the GSEs with much confidence or precision. The Treasury's support has reduced this risk, but it is not clear if stockholders will benefit.

Like all other businesses, the GSEs have *operational risk* due to the failure of internal controls. FHFA has directed the GSEs to reduce operational risk by improving their information technology, data quality, and internal controls.

As financial corporations, the GSEs are also subject to *model risk*, or the risk that their models (especially credit models) are not accurate. FHFA has directed the GSEs to update their financial models to reflect changing conditions.

What Is the Federal Government's Potential Contribution?

To keep the GSEs solvent from 2010 through 2012, Treasury has agreed to purchase as much senior preferred stock as necessary.[31]

---

[28] FHFA, pp. 30-36 and 46-51.

[29] A derivative is a financial contract whose value is linked to another financial instrument, price, or variable. For example, two companies could trade a derivative whose value was linked to the difference in the interest rates on 2-year and 10-year Treasury bonds.

[30] Board of Governors of the Federal Reserve System, "Current FAQs: What is the Federal Reserve's Maturity Extension Program?" press release, September 21, 2011, http://federalreserve.gov/faqs/money_15070.htm.

[31] U.S. Treasury, "Treasury Issues Update on Status of Support for Housing Programs," December 24, 2009, available at http://www.treasury.gov/press-center/press-releases/Pages/2009122415345924543.aspx.

Treasury initially had agreed to purchase a maximum of $100 billion in senior preferred stock from each GSE, and later increased the $100 billion to $200 billion.

After 2012, any unused portions of the $200 billion could be used.[32] Treasury's authority to amend the contracts expired December 31, 2009.[33]

Upon entering conservatorship (September 7, 2008), each GSE issued Treasury $1 billion of senior preferred stock and warrants (options) to purchase common stock. If the warrants are exercised, Treasury would own 79.9% of each company. As part of the contracts, each GSE has agreed to restrictions on paying dividends, issuing new stock, and disposing of assets.

At the same time as it increased its potential GSE support, Treasury increased the maximum retained portfolio that each GSE can hold. The maximum amount for each GSE is $900 billion as of December 31, 2009, and this maximum decreases by 10% annually until it reaches $250 billion. At this rate, it will take more than 12 years to reduce a GSE's portfolio to $250 billion. Previously, the ceiling was the actual size of the portfolio on December 31, 2009. By way of reference, at the end of 2010 Fannie Mae's retained mortgage portfolio was $789 billion and Freddie Mac's retained portfolio was $697 billion.

The December 24, 2009, announcement said that Treasury would terminate its program to purchase MBS of GSEs on December 31, 2009. Treasury estimated that at year end it held approximately $220 billion in MBS.[34] Treasury has said that it expects to profit from the spread between the interest rate that it pays to borrow money through bonds and the mortgage payments on the MBSs. Separately, the New York Federal Reserve had its own program to purchase $1.25 trillion of GSE and Ginnie Mae MBSs.[35] The GSEs will guarantee payment of the MBSs.

Treasury created a Government Sponsored Enterprise Credit Facility (GSECF) to provide liquidity to the GSEs, secured by MBSs pledged as collateral.[36] This facility terminated December 31, 2009.

Estimates of the total cost to the federal government use different baselines and vary widely. FHFA has estimated that by the end of 2014, Treasury is likely to purchase $220 billion-$311 billion of senior preferred stock[37] and the Congressional Budget Office has estimated the budget cost for "will exceed $300 billion."[38] Standard & Poor's has estimated that the total cost to

---

[32] More precisely, each the remaining balance of the $200 billion will be reduced by the positive net worth of the GSE on December 31, 2012.

[33] P.L. 111-5, §1117.

[34] U.S. Treasury, "Fact Sheet: GSE Mortgage Backed Securities Purchase Program," September 9, 2008, available at http://www.treasury.gov/press-center/press-releases/Documents/mbs_factsheet_090708hp1128.pdf.

[35] Federal Reserve Bank of New York, *FAQs: MBS Purchase Program*, March 24, 2009, available at http://www.newyorkfed.org/markets/mbs_FAQ.HTML.

[36] U.S. Treasury, "Fact Sheet: Government Sponsored Enterprise Credit Facility," September 7, 2008, available at http://www.treasury.gov/press-center/press-releases/Documents/gsecf_factsheet_090708.pdf.

[37] U.S. Federal Housing Finance Agency, "FHFA Updates Projections of Potential Draws for Fannie Mae and Freddie Mac," press release, October 27, 2011, http://www.fhfa.gov/webfiles/22737/GSEProjF.pdf.

[38] Congressional Budget Office, *The 2012 Long-Term Budget Outlook*, June 2012, p. 23, http://www.cbo.gov/sites/default/files/cbofiles/attachments/LTBO_One-Col_2.pdf.

resolve the GSEs could be $280 billion and that it would cost another $405 billion to capitalize a new entity or entities to replace Fannie Mae and Freddie Mac.[39]

What Risks Do Fannie Mae and Freddie Mac Create for the U.S. Government?

In the event of receivership, the usual priority of claims on remaining assets is administrative expenses of the receivership, senior and general debt, subordinated debt, and stock.[40] This would seem to place the MBSs with their guarantee at a fairly senior position, followed by GSE bonds, which would be ahead of the government's senior preferred stock, which would be ahead of all other stockholders.

If a GSE were to go into receivership, the value of its MBSs could decline because the value of the guarantee of timely payment of the MBSs would be called into question. If a GSE were unable to perform on the timely payment guarantee, the value of the MBSs would depend on the payment of the underlying mortgages, the rules of receivership, and the government's support for the MBSs.

The eventual value of the bonds would depend on the cause of the receivership and the details of the liquidation process. For example, if mortgage defaults and losses were to increase, the assets available for creditors would decrease.

In the event of receivership, it would appear unlikely that the senior preferred stock would have much value.

What is the Difference Between the Housing and Economic Recovery Act of 2008 and the Federal Housing Finance Regulatory Reform Act of 2008?

The Housing and Economic Recovery Act of 2008 is the title for the entire law, P.L. 110-289. The Federal Housing Finance Regulatory Reform Act of 2008 is the title for Title I-III of P.L. 110-289.

---

[39] Daniel E Teclaw and Vandana Sharma, *U.S. Government Cost To Resolve And Relaunch Fannie Mae And Freddie Mac Could Approach $700 Billion*, Standard & Poor's, November 4, 2010, p. 1, http://www2.standardandpoors.com/spf/pdf/events/FITcon11410Article4.pdf.

[40] CRS Report RL34657, *Financial Institution Insolvency: Federal Authority over Fannie Mae, Freddie Mac, and Depository Institutions*, by David H. Carpenter and M. Maureen Murphy contains more information on this subject.

Future

Could the GSEs Continue as Before?

In principle, Congress might decide that the changes that FHFA is making to each of the GSEs reduce the risk of future financial problems to an acceptable level and that the GSEs could return to stockholder control.[41]

The federal government's financial support extended to the GSEs could make a return to the prior status problematic. The elimination of dividends greatly reduced the value of the GSEs' preferred stock. Because the appeal of preferred stock is centered on the security of the dividend payments, the long-run value of their preferred stock has been reduced. The value of common stock has been reduced because of the termination of their dividends and increased uncertainty over the future long-run viability of the enterprises. Even if the GSEs were to return to stockholder control, it is not clear how much appeal their common and preferred stock would have for investors. If the GSEs were unable to raise capital, they would be unable to continue.

The treatment of bondholders could make lending to the GSEs more attractive. While common and preferred stockholders suffered during conservatorship (but not as much as they would have suffered from dissolution of the GSEs), payments to bond and MBS holders have continued as contracted. The government's actions could convince bondholders that the risk of holding bonds is less than previously thought. This would allow the GSEs to borrow money by selling bonds at rates very close to Treasury rates.

The increasing defaults and loss severity probably has made MBSs appear more risky, but the government's support of the GSEs could have offset this.

Once the housing market recovers, the GSEs could be in a very strong position to purchase mortgages and to create MBSs. For stockholders, the economics of the GSEs' mortgage business could be attractive, but the psychology of the decline in stock prices and the dividends on the senior preferred stock could potentially offset this plus.

One open question in the GSEs' return to stockholder ownership is the government's decision on what to do with the warrants for 80% of the GSEs' ownership. The government could auction the warrants off to the highest bidder, or the government could exercise the warrants to obtain control of the GSEs as each one's majority stockholder.

What Are Some of Congress's Options for Restructuring the GSEs?

Going forward, Congress has many options for reorganizing Fannie Mae and Freddie Mac, including (but not limited to) the following:

- Congress could make Fannie Mae and Freddie Mac part of the government. Both GSEs were originally government corporations, and this would be a return to that environment.

---

[41] See FHFA, pp. 21-52 for details on changes at Fannie Mae and Freddie Mac.

- Fannie Mae and Freddie Mac could become Federal Home Loan Banks. The 12 regional banks are a collective GSE that is owned by their member institutions, and their stock is not publicly traded. Fannie Mae's and Freddie Mac's stock could become an asset of the Federal Home Loan Bank System or of the individual banks.

- Fannie Mae and Freddie Mac could be split up into a large number of GSEs. Instead of two GSEs that are "too big to fail," there would be 10 or some other number of smaller GSEs that would arguably each be small enough to fail. The GSEs could be split in such a way that they would not be clones of each other and one or two could fail without the others going under. Congress might wish to explicitly state what the risks to stockholders, bondholders, and business partners would be. The competition could mean more benefits from GSE status go to homebuyers instead of the GSEs.

- Fannie Mae and Freddie Mac (and possibly additional new GSEs) could be converted into "utilities." These corporations would not necessarily be GSEs. Each could issue MBSs possibly guaranteed by the federal government, which would charge a fee for the guarantee. There are a number of options for how the fees could be set. The government could establish a standard fee, or it could auction off the right to issue a specific amount of MBSs. They could sell these MBSs or possibly retain them.

- The government could sell additional new GSE charters to the highest bidders.

- As then-Treasury Secretary, Henry M. Paulson, Jr. proposed using bonds backed not only by the issuing corporation's legal obligation of repayment, but also by the pledge of specific collateral as a way to allow banks to supplement, or even replace, the GSEs' role in mortgage markets.[42]

For additional information, see CRS Report R40800, *GSEs and the Government's Role in Housing Finance: Issues for the 112th Congress*, by N. Eric Weiss.

What Has Conservatorship Done to Stockholders and Other Stakeholders?

The powers of common stockholders, who formerly elected the boards of directors and approved certain enterprise actions, are suspended. FHFA as the conservator has assumed all of their authority. Previously, the common stockholders owned 100% of the GSEs. As a result of the warrants issued to the Treasury, they could own only 20% of the enterprises. In the long run, 20% of a healthy enterprise could be worth more than 100% of GSEs whose liabilities exceed their assets. In the short run, the price of the GSEs' common stock has declined, but if the GSEs recover, stockholders would arguably be better off compared to their situation at the time that conservatorship was undertaken.

---

[42] Henry M. Paulson, Jr., Secretary of the Treasury, "Remarks by Secretary Henry M. Paulson, Jr. on Recommendations from the President's Working Group on Financial Markets," press release, March 13, 2008, available at http://www.treasury.gov/press-center/press-releases/Pages/hp872.aspx. For more information about covered bonds, see CRS Report R41322, *Covered Bonds: Issues in the 112th Congress*, by Edward V. Murphy.

To the extent that current and former employees have invested in common stock, in the short run they have seen a decline in the value of their financial assets; the long-run outcome is not clear. Both GSEs had employee stock and option plans. The GSEs' agreements with Treasury prohibit issuing new stock. Consequently, those programs cannot continue until the GSEs emerge from conservatorship.

GSE employees have been urged by FHFA to continue working as before.

While the conservator is authorized by federal law to cancel certain contracts, FHFA has said that current contracts continue in force.

Treasury has purchased special senior preferred stock from Fannie Mae and Freddie Mac to maintain assets greater than liabilities. This senior preferred stock pays annual dividends of 10%, which would increase to 12% annually if a GSE fails to pay the dividend; these are the only dividends that the GSEs are allowed to pay. To date, the GSEs have increased the amount of preferred stock sold to Treasury to pay the dividends.

How Can Fannie Mae and Freddie Mac Leave Conservatorship?

There are two ways that Fannie Mae and Freddie Mac could exit their conservatorships. If they become financially viable, they could return to stockholder control. If they are unable to become financially viable, they could enter receivership. There is no legal reason that one GSE could not go into receivership and the other GSE return to stockholder control, although this might present some policy questions about the desirability of having a monopoly GSE.

There are several obstacles to a return to financial viability. In conservatorship, the GSEs are balancing their goals of support for home mortgage markets and their goal of profitability. At times, these goals may conflict. The concern of the federal government and FHFA for mortgage market stability and liquidity may take precedence over the return to profitability.[43]

The 10% cash or 12% senior preferred stock dividends owed to the federal government could be burdensome. The annual cash dividends of this stock equal or exceed the profits that the GSEs have earned in most years since 1998. This suggests that it could be difficult if not impossible for the GSEs to pay the required dividends without Treasury's continued financial support.

Context

What Is Conservatorship?

Conservatorship of Fannie Mae and Freddie Mac involves FHFA taking control of the GSEs. As conservator, the powers of the board of directors, officers, and shareholders are transferred to FHFA. A conservator can also cancel certain contracts. This is authorized by the Housing and

---

[43] Freddie Mac, *Form 10-K for the Fiscal Year Ending December 31*, p. 19, available at http://www.freddiemac.com/investors/er/pdf/10k_031109.pdf, and Fannie Mae, Form *10-K for the Fiscal Year Ending December 31, 2008*, p. 9, available at http://www.fanniemae.com/ir/pdf/earnings/2008/form10k_022609.pdf.

Economic Recovery Act of 2008 (HERA).[44] The goal of conservatorship is to preserve the GSE's assets and to return it to sound financial condition that would allow the conservatorship to be ended.

At the start of the conservatorships, FHFA replaced the CEOs of Fannie Mae and Freddie Mac.

Why Did the FHFA Place Fannie Mae and Freddie Mac Under Conservatorship?

As regulator of Fannie Mae and Freddie Mac, FHFA announced that it had placed Fannie Mae and Freddie Mac under conservatorship because of their deteriorating financial positions and the "critical importance" that each company has to the continued functioning of the residential financial markets.[45]

FHFA has said that continuing audits of the GSEs determined that their financial positions were weaker than previously thought and that the GSEs were unlikely to survive without conservatorship. FHFA cited previous public statements that the GSEs needed to increase their capital and needed to strengthen management controls over operations.

What Was Fannie Mae's and Freddie Mac's Financial Position?

In placing the GSEs under conservatorship, their new regulator, FHFA, has said that they need assistance to survive. FHFA reported that changes in the economy and the GSEs' slow recovery from their earlier accounting and financial problems reduced their financial strength.[46]

The Office of Federal Housing Enterprise Oversight (OFHEO), which was Fannie Mae's and Freddie Mac's safety and soundness regulator before July 30, 2008, repeatedly said that the GSEs had adequate capital.[47] In other words, according to OFHEO, the GSEs had sufficient funds to survive their financial difficulties.

This statement was difficult to verify independently. Details of the GSEs' portfolios and guarantees include confidential and proprietary information. In broad terms, the GSEs purchased slightly more than $169 billion of private label subprime MBSs in 2006 and 2007; they purchased slightly less than $58 billion of Alt-A MBSs in the same time period out of combined total mortgage purchases of $1.677 trillion.[48] At the end of 2007, the subprime and Alt-A MBSs represented 13.5% of the GSEs' total assets.

---

[44] P.L. 110-289, 122 Stat. 2654 et seq.

[45] Federal Housing Finance Agency, *Statement of FHFA Director James B. Lockhart*, September 7, 2008, available at http://www.fhfa.gov/webfiles/23/FHFAStatement9708final.pdf.

[46] Ibid.

[47] OFHEO, Statement of OFHEO Director James B. Lockhart, July 10, 2008, available at http://www.fhfa.gov/webfiles/1503/71008Statement.pdf.

[48] OFHEO, p. 113 and 116. Subprime and Alt-A MBS purchases prior to 2006 are not available.

Why Did Fannie Mae's and Freddie Mac's Stock Prices Decline in 2008?

Changes in the perception of the risks that Fannie Mae and Freddie Mac face—in terms of future profitability and even continued financial viability—reduced the price that investors are willing to pay for a share of the enterprises. There was also concern that intervention by the federal government would reduce the value of the common stock.

Between the end of 2007 and August 1, 2008, Fannie's stock lost 72% of its value, while Freddie's fell by 77%. Between the end of 2007 and September 30, 2008, Fannie Mae's market capitalization fell from $38.8 billion to $825 million, and Freddie Mac's capitalization declined from $26.8 billion to $473 million.[49] As part of the Treasury's financial aid package of September 7, 2008, the GSEs agreed to issue warrants to the Treasury worth 79.9% of their outstanding stock. If Treasury were to exercise the warrants, current stockholders would own 20% of each enterprise instead of 100%. This is one explanation why the GSEs' stock prices declined further since September 7, 2008.

Fannie Mae and Freddie Mac are GSEs whose charters limit them to buying single family and multifamily home mortgages originated by others. This lack of diversification makes them more exposed to housing and mortgage market problems than other financial institutions such as commercial banks that have other lines of business. The GSEs' charters give them a special relationship with the federal government, sometimes called an implicit guarantee, which has allowed them to borrow at interest rates only slightly above those paid by the federal government. In conservatorship, the GSEs have an even closer connection with the government.

The two GSEs were very highly leveraged versions of banks: they borrow money to purchase mortgages, and they maximize profits by keeping their capital reserves close to the minimum required by their regulators. Like banks, the GSEs are required by law and by their regulators to maintain a certain ratio between their loans and reserves to protect against loan losses. A key component of reserves is shareholders' equity or the current value of the shareholders' investments. Using funds for capital provides safety, but it is less profitable in normal times than purchasing additional mortgages.

Why Did FHFA Act on September 7, 2008, Instead of Earlier or Later?

FHFA, in general, followed the same approach that the Federal Deposit Insurance Corporation uses when it places a bank in conservatorship: a series of requests for changes to the corporation and increased capital followed by a sudden takeover. Providing a deadline could provide the regulated entity with an incentive to take risky gambles in a last attempt to avoid being seized by the government. The FDIC usually seizes a bank by suddenly showing up on a Friday afternoon, closing the bank, and locking the doors. This gives it time to make necessary changes over the weekend and resume business operations on the next business day.

---

[49] FHFA, pp. 121 and 138.

According to media reports at the time, some large foreign investors had been reducing their holdings of GSE debt, MBSs, and stock.[50] This would have made it more difficult for the GSEs to borrow money to finance their portfolios going forward. For example, Bank of China, Ltd. is reported to have sold or not replaced $4.6 billion of maturing GSE debt, which reduced its GSE debt holdings to $17.3 billion as of June 30, 2008. These same media reported that Treasury officials contacted foreign central banks and others to reassure them of the creditworthiness of GSE debt.

Are There Precedents for Placing Fannie Mae and Freddie Mac Under Conservatorship?

This is the first time that a GSE has been placed under conservatorship. It appears to also be the first time that the federal government has made a continuing commitment to a company (other than government corporations). On a more general level, the federal government has intervened in the past to assist many companies.[51] Since placing Fannie Mae and Freddie Mac under conservatorship, the federal government has intervened to support numerous companies, including General Motors, Chrysler, AIG, and various banks.[52]

Who Heads FHFA?

On August 6, 2009, FHFA Director James B. Lockhart announced that he would resign in the near future. President Obama named Senior Deputy Director for Housing Mission and Goals Edward J. DeMarco as acting director. On November 12, 2010, President Obama nominated Joseph A. Smith, North Carolina commissioner of banks, to be the FHFA director,[53] but the full Senate did not vote on his confirmation. The President has not made a new nomination for the position.

What Has Congress Done Previously to Improve the Financial Condition of the GSEs?

Congress has previously assisted GSEs that were in financial difficulty. When Fannie Mae was losing significant amounts of money in 1982, Congress passed the Miscellaneous Revenue Act of 1982 that provided tax benefits for Fannie Mae.[54] The Farm Credit System, another GSE, was aided with the Agricultural Credit Act of 1987, which authorized the issuance of $4 billion in bonds to support system members.[55]

---

[50] Deborah Solomon, Michael Corkery, and Liz Rappaport, "Mortgage Bailout Is Greeted With Relief, Fresh Questions," *Wall Street Journal*, September 9, 2008, p. A1.

[51] CRS Report RL34423, *Government Interventions in Financial Markets: Economic and Historic Analysis of Subprime Mortgage Options*, by N. Eric Weiss discusses some of these actions.

[52] CRS Report RS22956, *The Cost of Government Financial Interventions, Past and Present*, by Baird Webel, Marc Labonte, and N. Eric Weiss; also CRS Report R41427, *Troubled Asset Relief Program (TARP): Implementation and Status*, by Baird Webel.

[53] Office of the Press Secretary, The White House, "President Obama Announces More Key Administration Posts," press release, November 12, 2010, http://www.whitehouse.gov/the-press-office/2010/11/12/president-obama-announces-more-key-administration-posts.

[54] P.L. 97-362, 96 Stat. 1726 et seq.

[55] P.L. 100-233, 101 Stat. 1568 et seq.

Section 1117 of HERA authorizes the Treasury to purchase any amount of GSE securities—debt or equity—if necessary to provide stability to financial markets, prevent disruptions in the availability of mortgage credit, or protect the taxpayer.[56] This means that if either of the two GSEs becomes unable to raise funds in private markets, the federal government could simply purchase the debt securities that the firms were unable to sell elsewhere, or recapitalize either firm by purchasing stock, possibly becoming the majority shareholder. The authority to enter into new support contracts expired on December 31, 2009.

These contracts sent a signal to the markets that the Treasury was prepared to intervene rather than let either GSE fail.

What Other Actions Has the Federal Government Taken to Address the Financial Condition of the GSEs?

On July 15, 2008, the SEC issued an emergency order restricting short selling in the stock of 19 financial institutions, including Fannie and Freddie.[57] The SEC acted to prevent the possibility that false rumors could drive share prices down and cause the market to lose confidence, thereby cutting off the firms' access to credit markets, as happened to Bear Stearns in March 2008. The order restricting short sales of Fannie Mae and Freddie Mac stock was renewed on July 29, 2008, and expired on August 12, 2008.

The government has also taken steps to prepare for possible future support for the GSEs. On July 13, 2008, the Federal Reserve Board of Governors granted the New York Fed the authority to lend directly to the GSEs.[58] Section 1118 of HERA requires the new GSE regulator to consult with the Fed to ensure financial market stability.

In addition to the Fed's existing general authority to be a lender of last resort, the GSEs' charters give the GSEs a special relationship to the nation's central bank.[59] The Fed can use the GSEs' bonds purchased on the secondary market for open market operations.[60] This could indirectly help the GSEs by adding to the demand for their debt and increasing its liquidity. The Fed announced that it would conduct a special program to purchase GSE debt and MBS in calendar 2009 and the first quarter of 2010.[61] Under this program, the Fed purchased more than $1 trillion of GSE debt and GSE-issued MBS.

On September 21, 2011, the Federal Reserve's Open Market Committee decided to reinvest repayments of principal from agency debt and agency MBSs in agency MBSs.[62] In its last report

---

[56] H.R. 3221, P.L. 110-289, 122 Stat. 2654 et seq.

[57] http://www.sec.gov/rules/other/2008/34-58166.pdf.

[58] Federal Reserve Board of Governors, "Press Release," July 13, 2008, available at http://www.federalreserve.gov/newsevents/press/other/20080713a.htm.

[59] The Fed's lender of last resort authority is delineated at 12 U.S.C. 343. Fannie Mae's charter is at 12 U.S.C. 1716b et seq., and Freddie Mac's charter is at 12 U.S.C. 1401.

[60] 12 U.S.C. 347c.

[61] Federal Reserve Bank of New York, "FAQs: MBS Purchase Program," August 20, 2010, available at http://www.ny.frb.org/markets/mbs_faq.html.

[62] Federal Reserve Bank of New York, "FAQs: Reinvestments of Principal Payments on Agency Securities into Agency MBS," press release, January 31, 2012, http://www.newyorkfed.org/markets/ambs/ambs_faq.html. Agencies are guaranteed by Fannie Mae, Freddie Mac, and Ginnie Mae. Amounts reported are the unpaid principal balances of (continued...)

of the second quarter of 2012, the Fed reported that it held $863 billion of agency MBSs and $91 billion of agency debt.[63]

Who Has Invested in the GSEs?

There is little information available about who holds GSE stock, bonds, and MBSs. The Fed reports statistics for combined ownership of government agency and GSE debt and GSE MBSs. At the first quarter of 2012, non-U.S. investors held $999 billion of $7.5 trillion agency and GSE securities.[64] Other large investors were U.S.-chartered depository institutions ($1.7 trillion), life insurance companies ($387 billion), state and local government retirement funds ($290 billion), mutual funds ($1.0 trillion), and the GSEs themselves ($348 billion).

Fannie Mae reports that central bank ownership of certain types of debt declined from 41.1% at the end of 2008 to 15.6% as of May 21, 2012.[65] Freddie Mac showed central bank ownership of its debt declined from slightly less than 40% at the end of 2008 to 28% as of May 31 2012.[66]

What Recent Legislation Has Affected the GSEs?

Since the 110th Congress, five bills and two continuing resolutions have been signed into law that have had significant impacts on Fannie Mae, Freddie Mac, and the Federal Home Loan Banks.

In the 112th Congress, several bills, which have not become law, have been introduced to reform the GSEs. See CRS Report R41822, *Proposals to Reform Fannie Mae and Freddie Mac in the 112th Congress*, by N. Eric Weiss for information on these proposals. In addition, other legislation, discussed in CRS Report RS22172, *The Conforming Loan Limit*, by N. Eric Weiss and Sean M. Hoskins, has been introduced to permit the GSEs to purchase larger mortgages.

(...continued)

the underlying mortgages.

[63] Federal Reserve Bank of New York, "Federal Reserve Statistical Release H.4.4 Factors Affecting Reserve Balances of Depository Institutions and Condition Statement of Federal Reserve Banks," press release, June 28, 2012, http://www.federalreserve.gov/releases/h41/Current/.

[64] Federal Reserve, "Agency- and GSE-backed Securities," *Flow of Funds Accounts of the United States*, June 7, 2012, Table L. 210, available at http://www.federalreserve.gov/releases/z1/.

[65] Fannie Mae, "Noncallable Benchmark Notes Distribution Reports," *Benchmark Securities*, YTD 2012, available at http://www.fanniemae.com/resources/file/debt/pdf/benchmark-securities/2012_benchmark_distribution.pdf.

[66] Freddie Mac, *Freddie Mac Update*, June 2012, available at http://www.freddiemac.com/investors/pdffiles/investor-presentation.pdf.

Table 4. Public Laws Specifically Affecting GSEs

(Passed in 110th, 111th, and 112th Congresses)

P.L. Number	Date Enacted	Title	Summary
P.L. 110-185	February 13, 2008	Economic Stimulus Act of 2008 (ESA)	Increased conforming loan limits in high-cost areas for mortgages originated between July 1, 2007 and December 31, 2008.
P.L. 110-289	July 30, 2008	Housing and Economic Recovery Act of 2008 (HERA)	Created Federal Housing Finance Agency to replace Office of Federal Housing Enterprise Oversight as combined GSE regulator. Made high-cost area conforming loan limits permanent, but at lower amounts.
P.L. 111-5	February 7, 2009	American Recovery and Reinvestment Act of 2009 (ARRA)	Extended 2008 high-cost conforming loan limits to 2009 mortgages.
P.L. 111-88	October 30, 2009	Department of Interior Appropriations Act for FY2010	Extended 2008 high-cost conforming loan limits for FY2010.
P.L. 111-242	September 30, 2010	Continuing Appropriations Act of 2011	Extended 2008 high-cost conforming loan limits for FY2011.
P.L. 112-78	December 23, 2011	Temporary Payroll Tax Cut Continuation Act of 2011	Requires Fannie Mae and Freddie Mac to increase their guarantee fees by 10 basis points and the funds raised are to be deposited in the Treasury.
P.L. 112-105	April 4, 2012	Stop Trading on Congressional Knowledge Act of 2012	Prohibition on bonuses to executives of Fannie Mae and Freddie Mac while they are in conservatorship.

Source: The Congressional Research Service.

Glossary

Alt-A mortgage	Either a mortgage made to a borrower with a credit history between prime and subprime, or a mortgage made to a prime borrower with less than traditional documentation.
ARRA	American Recovery and Reinvestment Act of 2009, P.L. 111-5, 123 Stat. 115.
ESA	Economic Stimulus Act of 2008, P.L. 110-185, 122 Stat. 613,
FHFA	Federal Housing Finance Agency. Regulator of housing GSEs for mission, safety and soundness. Created by merger of existing government agencies, including OFHEO and HUD staff (who formerly had mission regulatory authority).
GSE	Government-sponsored enterprise.
GSECF	Government-sponsored enterprise credit facility. The Treasury's program to lend money to Fannie Mae, Freddie Mac, and the Federal Home Loan Banks using MBS as collateral. This program expired December 31, 2009, and was authorized by HERA.
HERA	Housing and Economic Recovery Act of 2008, P.L. 110-289, 122 Stat. 2654.
MBSs	Mortgage-backed securities. A pool of mortgages sold to institutional investors.
OFHEO	Office of Federal Housing Enterprise. Safety and soundness regulator for Fannie Mae and Freddie Mac. Merged into Federal Housing Finance Agency.
prime mortgage	A mortgage made to a borrower with excellent credit history.
private-label MBSs	Mortgage-backed securities underwritten and sold by commercial and investment banks. They are not created by the GSEs or a government agency.
senior preferred stock	This stock is senior to (has priority over) all other common and preferred stock; it is the only GSE stock currently receiving dividends.
subprime mortgage	A mortgage made to a borrower with a blemished credit history.

Author Contact Information

N. Eric Weiss
Specialist in Financial Economics
eweiss@crs.loc.gov, 7-6209

www.ingramcontent.com/pod-product-compliance
Lightning Source LLC
Chambersburg PA
CBHW081246180526
45171CB00005B/564